Joe's Big Backhoe Adventure:
A True Tale from Flint
Marcy Schaaf

In Michigan, there are specific rules regarding the operation of farm equipment. Generally, a standard driver's license is **not required** for driving tractors and other farm equipment on public roads, as long as the vehicle is being used for agricultural purposes, such as moving from one site to another. However, the equipment must have a slow-moving vehicle sign, flashing lights, and other safety features to ensure visibility and safety on the road.

For other types of farm vehicles, such as trucks, the requirements can vary based on weight and usage. Vehicles weighing over 26,000 pounds or used for transporting hazardous materials typically require a commercial driver's license.

While it is generally legal for farm equipment to be driven **without** a standard driver's license, it is essential to follow safety regulations and ensure that young operators, especially those under 16, are adequately trained.
Please keep this in mind while reading this true story!

In Flint, Michigan,
there lived a 10-year-old boy named Joe.

Joe's dad, Charlie,
owned an excavating business.
Schaaf and Davis
Excavating
3201 Starkweather St Flint. MI 48506
742-5083

Joe and his three brothers
helped during summer.

One day, Joe's dad gave him a big job.

"Drive the backhoe
across town to the job site," said Dad.

Joe, excited,
climbed into the big backhoe.

He started the engine and began
driving carefully.

**Halfway across town
a police officer saw Joe.**

The officer stopped Joe and asked,
"How old are you?"

Joe replied,
"I'm 10. I need to get to the job site."

The officer looked surprised
but decided to help.

"I'll follow you," said the officer kindly.

Joe continued driving,
with the police car behind him.

They drove through the town,
passing many curious faces.

Finally,
they arrived at the construction site.

Charlie's face turned red when he saw the police car.

Charlie approached the officer
and Joe quickly.

"Why did you stop my son?"
asked Charlie.

He's a bit young to be driving heavy equipment Mr. Schaaf

He doesn't need a license for this farm equipment: Charlie Said

Charlie smiled and patted
Joe on the back.

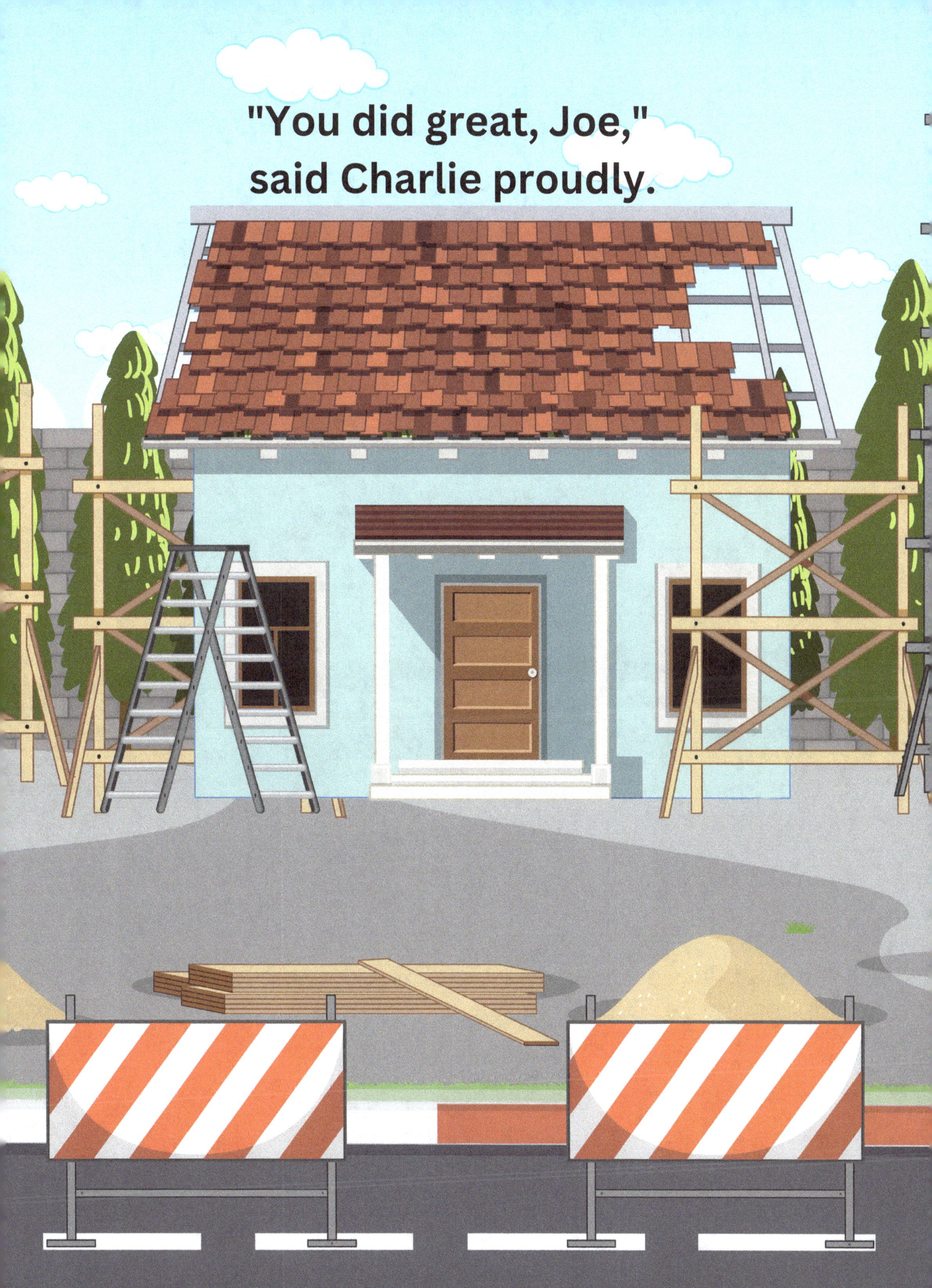
"You did great, Joe,"
said Charlie proudly.

Joe felt proud and happy
for completing his task.

The officer smiled and drive away.

From that day, Joe felt more confident.

Joe was a good driver and he loved
helping his dad with the business.

Driving the backhoe was
Joe's favorite job.

Charlie trusted Joe even more after that day.

Joe and his brothers enjoyed
their summer work.

Every summer, they made more happy memories together.

The End.

In Flint, Michigan, farm equipment generally includes a variety of tools and machinery used in agricultural operations. This encompasses items such as tractors, plows, harvesters, and irrigation systems. These types of equipment are essential for various farming tasks like planting, cultivating, and harvesting crops.

According to the information I found, specific types of farm equipment can range from manual tools to large machinery. Common examples include:

Tractors - Used for plowing, tilling, and other heavy-duty farm tasks.
Combines - Machines that harvest, thresh, and clean grain crops.
Plows - Tools used to turn over the soil in preparation for planting.
Harrows - Devices used to break up and level soil.
Irrigation Systems - Equipment used to supply water to crops.
It's important to note that certain pieces of heavy equipment, such as backhoes and skid steers, while often used in both agricultural and construction contexts, can also be considered part of farm equipment due to their versatile applications in farm operations

Books By Schaaf

www.BookBySchaaf.com

Find us at: